LEARN TO

LOUGHBOROUGH COLLEGE

LEARN TO
WINDSURF

Farrel O'Shea

Revised by Bill Dawes

WARD LOCK

A WARD LOCK BOOK

First published in the UK 1997
by Ward Lock
Wellington House
125 Strand
LONDON
WC2R OBB

A Cassell Imprint

Distributed in the United States
by Sterling Publishing Co., Inc.
387 Park Avenue South, New York, NY 10016–8810

A British Library Cataloguing in Publication Data block for this book may be obtained from the British Library

ISBN 0 7063 7541 6
Typeset by Keystroke, Jacaranda Lodge, Wolverhampton
Printed and bound in Great Britain by Bath Press

METRIC CONVERSION TABLE	
1 millimetre (mm)	= 0.03 inch
1 centimetre (cm)	= 0.39 inch
1 metre (m)	= 1.09 yards, 3.28 feet
1 square metre (m²)	= 1.196 square yards
1 kilometre (km)	= 0.62 mile
1 gram (g)	= 0.03 ounce
1 kilogram (kg)	= 2.20 pounds
1 litre	= 1.76 pints

Contents

1 HISTORY AND DEVELOPMENT OF WINDSURFING

Within a few decades windsurfing has evolved from an obscure minority sport into perhaps the most popular water sport in the world. Windsurfing has no climatic or topographical boundaries – where there is water, there is windsurfing. Armed with some basic knowledge, one can quickly experience the joys of sailing, coupled with the thrills and spills of surfing. It is not very difficult to see why there are now millions of participants worldwide.

BEGINNINGS

The origins of windsurfing go back to 1958, when British inventor Peter Chilvers came up with what seemed rather an eccentric idea: a sailing rig joined to a board by a free-moving 'universal joint'. He built and used his device, but did not take the idea any further. However, Jim Drake, an American friend of Chilvers, witnessed the idea. Many years later, when Drake had returned to California, he decided to see if something similar could be put into production. Drake's friend Hoyle Schweitzer helped him to overcome the many technical hitches involved in the design. A United States Patent application was soon made for the appropriately named 'Windsurfer' (Figure 1). Drake and Schweitzer then risked a small production run, initially supplying their friends. The Windsurfer did not initially sell to expectations, so Schweitzer bought Drake out of his half of the patent for what, with

Nothing beats the exhilaration of blasting across the water at speed.

Figure 1 The original Windsurfer.

hindsight, appears to have been a nominal fee.

With true Californian entrepreneurial spirit, Schweitzer tried to protect his investment by registering the patent in as many countries as possible. Sales suddenly took a sharp upward turn, and the new Californian toy attracted European interest. A Dutch company, Ten Cate, began importing into Europe, and the Windsurfer soon took off in Holland, Germany and France. By 1973, the parent company could not keep up with demand, so Ten Cate began to manufacture in Europe under licence. Within a couple of years many other European plastic manufacturers realized the potential and set up rival – albeit unlicensed – production. All the boards were very similar in shape and design to the original Windsurfer, but far cheaper! Lengthy court wrangles followed, and most manufacturers resigned themselves to paying Schweitzer's 7.5 per cent patent fee.

However, Bic, the French plastics company, was very keen for a slice of the windsurfing market. They heard about Peter Chilvers and his original invention, and brought him back onto the scene in their court action to get the Schweitzer patent overturned. Bic won the case, and the Schweitzer patent was revoked in Europe, allowing the manufacturing floodgates to open. Europe soon established itself as the main manufacturing base, while Schweitzer eventually disappeared from the scene. To this day all the biggest and most successful brands still hail from France and Germany.

COMPETITIONS

As the sport expanded, the competitive side of windsurfing quickly developed. As no one really had any better ideas at the time, it inevitably adopted a similar format to dinghy and yacht racing. However, it soon became apparent that the original Windsurfer and all similar designs had drawbacks on the long upwind legs favoured by the traditional yacht-racing 'triangle' course. Boards with deeper, more rounded hulls, which worked more on the principle of a yacht, were developed for triangle racing. These boards performed so much better in light airs that it became necessary to divide the fleet into two categories. Flat-bottomed boards like the Windsurfer were now classed as Division I, a category for the recreational sailor. Division II, with its rounded 'displacement' boards (which went upwind very well, but were extremely unstable and required more skill to sail), was tailored more for the serious racer.

DESIGN IMPROVEMENTS

Meanwhile, in Hawaii, with its strong, constant trade winds and big waves, designers were beginning to develop boards that could be used surfboard-style. The traditional Windsurfer design was difficult to control in Hawaii's demanding conditions, particularly while heading out through big waves, when the rider would often become airborne and separated from the board in the process. In late 1977, two Hawaiian sailors, Mike Horgan and Larry Stanley, solved this problem by fitting footstraps to their boards. This invention changed the face of windsurfing and introduced the 'funboard' style of windsurfer to everyone. With the advantage of footstraps, control became easier, and more challenging conditions could be attempted.

As sailors started to venture out in bigger waves and stronger winds, board design had to undergo some radical changes. Daggerboards were designed to be retracted fully into the hull or dispensed with completely, and boards were steered by a combination of rig and foot pressure through the straps, surfboard-style. The new reliance on foot steering led to the development of the high-speed 'carve gybe' turn.

Custom board manufacture soon became popular, as sailors built boards to their own requirements and ideas. With the much smaller boards now being built, sailors could jump waves and maintain a modicum of control while airborne. Stories and pictures of the Hawaiian wave-jumpers soon spread to Europe, and funboard mass-production hit the European market. Sail and rig technology developed alongside the new board shapes at a similar rate. The old triangular rigs were modified to suit the surf and the new, more manoeuvre-oriented style of sailing. Booms were shortened, and the clew, or back end of the sail, was raised to avoid the breaking waves.

In Hawaii's consistent trade winds, the 'water-start' manoeuvre evolved as an efficient and labour-saving alternative to standing on the board and uphauling the sail. In the water-start, the wind does all the work, effortlessly pulling the sailor up from the water and onto the board. The new, more stable higher-aspect sails were prerequisites for such fancy new moves. Performance gains from these new boards and sails were so great that, almost overnight, a great deal of windsurfing hardware became obsolete. Demand for the latest high-tech kit was massive, and the sport and its associated industry multiplied apace.

'Radical' is the only word to describe

subsequent developments. With the water-start technique, early stars such as Mike Waltze and Robby Naish now found they could use boards that were too small and sinky to uphaul conventionally. The water-start-only boards, or 'sinkers' as they became known, were lighter and more manoeuvrable, allowing even more extreme moves and tricks to be developed. Many sailors took to cutting down large surfboards to the dimensions of the new-style windsurfing waveboards.

After a visit to Maui, Hawaii, a leading German sailor called Jurgen Honscheid returned to Europe with one of these converted surfboards. At the 1981 Weymouth speed trials he delighted the crowd by his turn of speed and sweeping carved gybes. It was not long before the traditional Division I and II boards were pushed aside by the new generation of

With the proper tuition and specially designed lightweight equipment, children can learn to windsurf with remarkable ease.

funboards, especially as they could also be raced! Funboard racing in stronger winds became the new craze. Courses were modified extensively, with shortened upwind legs and long-reaching legs. The funboard also gave birth to slalom racing, a completely new discipline with no upwind legs, just high-speed reaches and fast downwind turns.

The year 1984 was a watershed in windsurfing, as the sport was granted Olympic status for the first time. However, the Olympic rules required a board design that was well established and internationally available, which led to the unfortunate decision to use the

'Windglider' Division I board. In 1984, the Windglider was already obsolete in comparison to the funboards everyone was now sailing.

Hawaii continued to strengthen its position as the research and development capital of the windsurfing world with the introduction of fully battened sails. It was not a new idea (Chinese junks had fully battened sails 2,000 years ago), but worked particularly well on a windsurfing sail. Full-length battens increased the sail's stability, and boom lengths could be shortened further. This made the sail easier to handle and control, allowing sailors to ride bigger waves and maintain control in stronger winds.

Using these Hawaiian innovations to full advantage, Maui sailor Fred Haywood, using a sail with extra battens below the boom and a wing-foiled mast, shattered the 30-knot barrier at Weymouth speed week in 1986. Although the top speeds are now almost half as fast again, this is still regarded as one of the sport's great milestones – the 'four-minute mile' of windsurfing.

For the next few years most of the exciting developments were in sail design, as manufacturers concentrated on increasing sail stability and performance. The fully battened sail soon led to the Rotating Aspect Foil (RAF) sail and the camber-inducer. Then followed almost a decade of refinement, with some design 'red herrings' appearing. However, although the boards and sails available in the early 1990s did not look much different to those of the mid-1980s, the general performance on offer was much higher.

THE WORLD CUP

By now the sport had become much more professional and organized. A thriving World Cup professional race circuit was in force, comprising teams from most of the major manufacturers. The World Cup events became hugely popular, particularly in Europe, where crowds of 100,000 and more would turn out to see their heroes in action.

To capitalize on the sport's visual impact and

The carve gybe.

excitement, indoor windsurfing was born. A flooded arena, equipped with a row of wind-generating electric fans, saw slalom racing and jumping contests for the top World Cup sailors. The first indoor events were held at the Bercy stadium in Paris, and were an amazing success. Coupled with fireworks, rock music, guest appearances by other stars and slick presentation, the televized shows met with a rapturous reception. Indoor windsurfing has now spread to many other countries, but Bercy is still regarded as the biggest and best of the shows.

The World Cup circuit was where all the best board and sail designers were working, and the major source of research and development for the sport. Unfortunately, this meant that, while equipment for racing was improving every year, recreational equipment was not changing very much at all.

RECENT DEVELOPMENTS

Windsurfing's next major period of development started in 1992, when fin manufacturers began to use the latest materials and construction technology to produce narrow 'blade' fins. Although blade fins are now commonplace, at the time they were an incredible breakthrough, capable of powering a board to high speeds without becoming uncontrollable.

The high speeds, high manoeuvrability and high control offered by blade fins led directly to the next milestone in board development. Designers found that by moving the board's widest point much further rearwards they could achieve further increases in manoeuvrability with no loss of speed. This resulted in boards with a pronounced 'teardrop' plan shape, rather than the traditional 'lollipop stick' shape. Consequently, just about every board built since 1994 has been of teardrop outline, and very much of the funboard variety.

The evolution of new manoeuvres and techniques has occurred at a much more steady pace over the last 10–12 years. For many years sailors had been trying to develop the basic jump into something more radical. By 1986 a few top sailors were performing the 'backward

loop', a 360° rotation of board, sail and sailor. An even higher percentage of sailors were simply crashing in a variety of interesting ways! The situation changed completely in the winter of 1987, when Italian World Cup wave sailor Cesare Cantagalli invented the 'cheese roll', which was the first ever forward loop. Cheese rolls also differed from the backward loop in that they were performed downwind, not upwind. Every proficient short-board sailor was soon attempting cheese rolls, with varying degrees of success. Never have so many broken noses been sustained during one short season.

The cheese roll has now evolved into more of a cartwheeling rotation, neither upwind nor downwind but purely 'end-over-end', and is simply called a 'forward'. Performed high and fast, it is without question one of the most spectacular windsurfing manoeuvres ever, but progress has not stopped there. Sailors now loop one-handed, even one-footed, or leave the rotation as late as possible – the 'stalled forward'. Loops are also being coupled with other aerial moves, creating combination manoeuvres such as the 'table-top forward'. As equipment and skills continue to improve, ever more radical variations are being attempted. Double forward loops are now commonplace, and a few sailors are even attempting triples.

However, this is all far removed from the sport as it is known by most of its followers. Perfect wave conditions are rare, and for 99 per cent of sailors windsurfing means pottering about on a long board in light winds, or charging about on a long or short board in stronger winds.

The sport has now come of age, and is backed in most countries by professional organizations and well-managed, well-structured teaching systems. Equipment has improved to the point where it is commonplace for people to progress from complete beginners to competent high-wind sailors in one season. Good equipment, recognized schools, books, magazines and videos all help to ease the pains of learning, and bring the pleasures of this exciting sport within the reach of everyone.

The water-start.

2 EQUIPMENT AND TECHNOLOGY

A casual observer, glancing along the beach on a breezy summer's day, will be struck by the variety of boards on display. Makes and models obviously differ, but there are also differences in size, shape, colour and method of construction.

CONSTRUCTION

The materials used and methods of construction have an important bearing on price and performance. By far the cheapest construction method is 'blow-moulding' in polyethylene and/or polypropylene (the type of plastic washing-up bowls are made of), which lends itself well to mass-production around a foam core. Boards of this material are very robust and will withstand a lot of stress both on and off the water. However, if they are damaged (which is very rare) they are difficult to repair at home.

The other main method of board construction uses a composite skin of fibreglass-based materials, often including exotic materials such as carbon and kevlar. This is heat-sealed ('thermoformed') with epoxy resin onto a lightweight foam core in a steel mould. Composite construction produces a lighter and stiffer board with a smoother finish than blow-moulding, but is a more expensive process. The material is a little more susceptible to damage, but easier to repair than polyethylene. Composite construction is found on just about

The carve gybe is hard to master, but it is the fastest and most satisfying way of turning a short board.

all high-performance production boards, and most manufacturers have a choice of different composite builds, which vary in weight, durability and expense to suit all wallets and requirements.

True performance freaks often prefer to have a board that is custom-made to their own specification. Instead of using a mould, the custom board-producer will handshape the foam core and then envelop it in fibreglass and resin. This handbuilt approach is time-consuming and labour-intensive, but no more expensive than most production-based composite boards. Custom production is usually only used for fairly specialist short boards, generally for wave-sailing or racing.

Both custom and production manufacturers can now offer boards built in 'sandwich' construction, where a thin strip of hard foam (or occasionally high-tech 'honeycomb' material) is used below the outer skin for greatly increased strength and stiffness. Manufacturers are experimenting with many different types of foam and construction processes, leading to high-performance short boards that weigh less than 6 kg in total.

DESIGN

While the construction obviously plays a large part in how a board performs, it is the design that really makes the difference, and there is an incredible array of shapes and sizes on offer. Boards are made in just about every length between 380 cm and 250 cm, and widths vary from a sleek 47 cm on the most speed-oriented designs, through to a massive 75 cm+ on the most stable beginner boards. Essentially, the

Figure 2 Board and rig components.

Plan view – the positioning of the footstraps, mast wells and daggerboard cassette is a primary consideration in board manufacture.
(a) Towing eye. *(b)* Mast track. *(c)* Daggerboard. *(d)* Daggerboard cassette. *(e)* Footstraps. *(f)* Fin bolt. *(g)* Deckpads.

(a) Head of the sail. *(b)* Roach – the area outside a line between head and clew. *(c)* Leech of the sail. *(d)* Sail clew – reinforced with metal eyelet. *(e)* Outhaul fixing – the clew of the sail is attached to the back of the boom with a rope threaded through a pulley system and tied off with a cleat on the boom. *(f)* Boom (variable length). *(g)* Foot of the sail. *(h)* Foot roach – the area outside a line between foot and clew. *(i)* Downhaul – the tack of the sail is tensioned through the mast extension or foot with a pulley system and tied off with a cleat. *(j)* Deckpads – under each footstrap to increase grip and comfort. *(k)* Footstraps – a choice of fixing positions is usually offered. *(l¹)* Finbolt – most boards have a bolt-through fin-fixing system. *(l²)* Fin-box. *(l³)* Fin. *(m)* Tail. *(n)* Daggerboard slot – reinforced and built into the hull. *(o)* Retractable daggerboard. *(p)* Nose – all production boards come fitted with a towing eye, and occasionally a rubber bumper too. *(q)* Towing eye. *(r)* Mast track – some boards have a sliding mast track that can be operated while sailing. *(s)* Mast foot and universal joint. *(t)* Uphaul – knotted to give grip. *(u)* Boom clamp. *(v)* Boom cutout. *(w)* Mast – made from fibreglass and carbon. *(x)* Luff of the sail. *(y)* Battens – fixed into batten pockets. *(z)* Mast head.

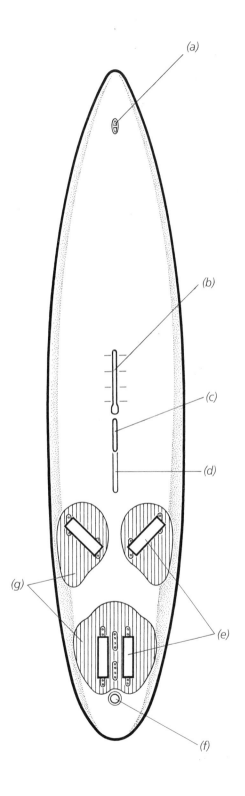

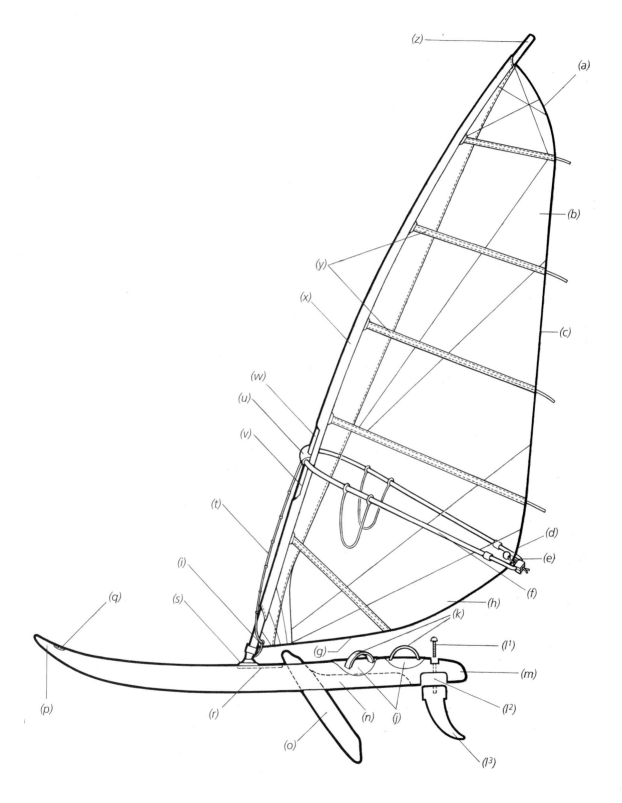

longer and wider the board is the more stable it is, and thus more suitable for a beginner and/or use in light winds. The shorter it gets the more proficient the sailor needs to be.

Volume determines the board's flotation, and it is measured in litres. Again, the higher the volume, the easier the board is to sail. Beginners' boards are often about 250 litres, while an out-and-out waveboard may be down to as little as 75 litres. The heavier the sailor the more volume is required to keep him afloat.

While length, width and bulk (volume) offer the most obvious differences, the more subtle parameters of plan shape, rocker line, rail shape and underwater profile are also vitally important. Plan shape, and in particular the position of the widest point, affects the board's manoeuvrability. Placing the point of maximum width forward makes the board more directionally stable. If it is moved further back the board will be more manoeuvrable.

The curve or rocker line of the hull affects manoeuvrability and speed. A board with a shallow rocker, such as a racing board, will have great speed and plane early, but is more difficult to turn and jump than something with a more banana-like rocker line, as found on waveboards. The height of the nose (the 'scoop' rocker) determines how easily the board will cut through waves, chop and swell.

Rail shape affects the way a board grips the water. Thick, slab-sided rails, usually with a sharp 'corner' at the bottom, are quick to plane and good upwind, but can be difficult to gybe as they can lose grip easily. A soft rail has better gripping qualities, but is not as fast or as quick to plane.

As for underwater profiles, most modern hulls incorporate a certain amount of vee, often just in the tail. Like the keel of a boat, vee helps the board cut through the water, giving increased directional stability and a smooth ride. Vee in the nose can also help the board cut through chop and waves. Other than that, the underside of the board is usually fairly flat, allowing it to track as smoothly through and over the water as possible.

Clearly, board design is not as simple as it may at first appear. A change of as little as 1 cm in any of the above variables can radically alter a board's behaviour. Fortunately, it is not necessary to know the exact measurements for every parameter if you are looking for a new board. The market can be subdivided into fairly distinct categories. There are many different levels of performance available, so be careful to purchase according to your needs and ability level. Do not be tempted into buying a Ferrari before you have learned to drive. If you buy a board that is too high-tech you will make life very difficult for yourself, and potentially waste a lot of money. Below are a few of the main categories that you are likely to find on your local beach.

TYPES OF BOARD

BEGINNER BOARD The most basic board of all. Long, high-volume, usually in blow-moulded construction, unencumbered by footstraps and complex fittings, and designed for maximum stability, durability and low cost. These boards are great to learn on, and you will find them at any windsurfing school, but they are not ideal for stronger winds or more advanced sailing.

INTERMEDIATE/MID-LENGTH BOARDS Boards between 320 cm and 350 cm are designed to offer relatively good performance in light/medium winds. They work well for inexperienced sailors, but also offer a modicum of performance in stronger winds. These all-round funboards are ideal for anyone looking to learn more advanced techniques, or those who want something that will work reasonably well in all conditions.

RACEBOARDS Very long and high in volume, these specialist machines are a cross between the old Division I and Division II boards, and are used for racing in just about any wind strength. Raceboards can carry a very

Just a small selection of boards available from one manufacturer. Left to right: 328-cm beginner/inter-mediate board; 278-cm slalom board; 265-cm wave/slalom board; 258-cm waveboard. Note the modern 'teardrop' outline.

big sail for maximum power in light airs, and are thus the fastest thing going in light/medium winds. However, they are very expensive and bristle with footstraps and fittings, so despite their monster size they are not ideal for inexperienced sailors.

SHORT BOARDS Anything under around 3 m in length is really too short to include a daggerboard, and is officially a 'short board'. Short boards can only be used in planing conditions, which means winds of 10 knots and above. Planing occurs when there is enough power to drive the board up 'onto the plane', so it is skimming over the water's surface like a water-ski, rather than ploughing through it like a boat.

Short boards come in many categories to cater for every recreational and racing requirement. The bigger short boards (285–300 cm) are for use in the lighter planing winds. For stronger winds there is a very wide choice of 'slalom boards' in the 265–285 cm range. All offer different combinations of recreational and racing capabilities, speed, comfort, and manoeuvrability. Anything smaller than 265 cm is a specialist design for very high winds, either for wave sailing or out-and-out speed.

FITTINGS AND FIXTURES

The first boards had a built-in fin, and a simple hole in the deck for fixing the mast. The daggerboard slotted straight into the fully extended position. If you wanted less daggerboard in stronger winds, you had to pull it out by hand by the carrying handle, and hook it over your shoulder! Nowadays, the fittings are much more sophisticated. Here are the main features you are likely to find on a modern windsurfing board.

FOOTSTRAPS Footstraps (Figure 3) are only needed in planing conditions, when they help in steering, and also keep the sailor in contact with the board in choppy waters. For the beginner, footstraps are merely something to trip over. They impede the learning process, and are not necessary in light winds. Although

Figure 3 Footstrap.

beginner boards are usually supplied with straps, they should be removed until the time is right.

Boards intended for intermediates will usually have a wide choice of footstrap-fixing positions. Bringing the straps further back on the board increases speed, but makes the board more difficult to control. It is best to start with the straps as far forward as possible, and then bring them further aft as competence and confidence improves.

Do not try to get your whole foot into the strap. Most footstraps are adjustable in size, usually by means of Velcro tongues or a buckle system situated beneath the soft exterior cover. For safety and comfort the strap must be correctly adjusted so it fits comfortably over the bridge of the foot. Having the strap too loose could result in a twisted ankle or worse mishap.

DAGGERBOARDS The daggerboard, which fits in a slot just behind the mast, is found on all longer boards. When lowered, it greatly increases the stability of the board, and is also an indispensable aid for upwind work, especially in light airs. In strong winds the daggerboard creates too much lift and makes the board very difficult to control. This is why daggerboards are designed to pivot fore and aft, and can retract fully up into the hull when necessary.

Daggerboards vary in size, with the larger variety being found in race boards, where upwind ability is most important. All-round funboards have shorter, narrower daggerboards, which are perfectly adequate for stability in light winds, and offer reasonable upwind performance. On boards smaller than around 320 cm, daggerboards become redundant, as such designs are intended for strong-wind work only, when a daggerboard is not required, even for going upwind.

MAST TRACKS All modern boards have some form of mast-track system, giving the scope to position the mast foot further fore or aft on the board, depending on the wind or the point of sailing.

In light airs, the board will plane earlier if the mast foot is positioned forwards. A forward position will also feel more comfortable when big sails with longer boom lengths are used. A forward mast-foot position is better for going upwind as the board's effective waterline length is increased. As the wind picks up, the board will perform better with the mast foot placed further aft. If in doubt, leave the mast foot positioned fairly centrally in its track, and experiment from there.

On a raceboard you need to be able to adjust the mast-foot position while on the move, for maximum performance on any point of sailing.

Therefore, raceboards and some all-round funboards have a sliding track that can be operated by a foot pedal while sailing. Shorter boards usually have a simple fin-box track fitting into which the mast foot is fixed via a 'deck plate'. This can be repositioned in the fin-box track easily by hand, but not while sailing.

FINS The fin provides directional stability, and balances the sideways force generated by the sail. Without a fin the board just will not steer! In planing conditions it is very important to make sure the fin is compatible with the size of sail you are using. Consequently, just like sails, fins come in a range of shapes and sizes. Bigger and more upright fins create more lift, but are

A range of fins, including blade, swept-back, and wave models. The type and size of fin you use will depend on the board you are sailing, and on the wind and water conditions.

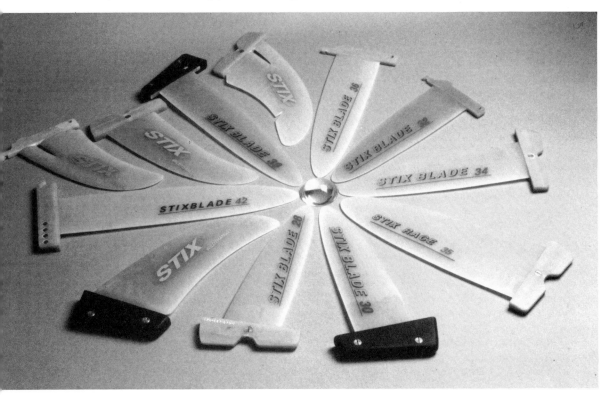

not very manoeuvrable. Smaller, swept-back fins create less lift, are more forgiving and make the board easier to turn.

Generally, the larger the board the larger the fin needs to be. Larger fins work well in light winds as they can counteract the force of the big sail often used in such airs. They also give lots of lift, making them particularly good for going upwind, and will be found on all boards designed for course racing.

As winds pick up, board speeds increase, and the amount of lift generated by the fin increases. A smaller fin is therefore better suited to stronger airs, and for wave sailing when maximum manoeuvrability is required, the fin will be both small and swept-back.

Foil shape also affects a fin's performance. Like sails, fuller-foiled fins generate more lift, and offer better acceleration. Flatter-profiled fins create less lift, but they do not produce as much drag and allow a higher top speed.

Most modern boards offer a 'bolt-through' fin-box system, by which the fin fits into a box underneath the board, and is fixed by a bolt in the upper deck.

Fins are quite expensive, as they are usually made of high-tech, epoxy resin-based construction, often including carbon or kevlar. Plastic fins, although cheaper, are very flexible, and lead directly to spin-out. Spin-out occurs when planing. Bubbles travel down the fin, causing it to lose grip in the water, and directional stability is suddenly lost.

SAILS The theory of forward motion by wind and sail power is quite simple (Figure 4). As wind flows towards the sail it separates at the mast and travels along each side of the sail. Owing to the curvature of the sail, the wind affects each side differently. On the leeward side the air is accelerated (as it has further to go), resulting in a pressure reduction, while on the windward side the air slows down, creating a high-pressure zone. This action of high pressure pushing against low pressure creates the drive necessary to propel the craft forwards.

The natural direction of this force will push the board sideways and forwards. It is the function of the daggerboard and/or fin, along with the general shape and lines of the board,

to resist this sideways push and ensure that there is forward motion with minimal lateral drift.

Most new boards are sold with a sail between 5.5 and 6 m², which is an ideal all-round size. However, when the wind increases it becomes physically difficult to hold such a big sail. When this happens it is time to change down to a smaller, more manageable size. In very light winds (and/or for more power and speed) you may wish to 'change up' to a bigger sail size. Consequently, most manufacturers offer sails in a variety of styles, ranging from a 3-m² handkerchief up to a monster 9 m². These extreme sizes are for specialist use only, with the 'handkerchiefs' intended for high-wind wave-sailors, and the mega sails for light-wind racing. Choice of sail sizes will depend on where you sail, the winds you sail in, the sort of board you sail and your bodyweight. A heavier sailor needs more power, while a smaller sailor needs something easier to control.

The windsurfing sail consists of a series of shaped panels taped and sewn together. The main body is generally made of clear monofilm panels, while Dacron and/or Mylar cloth is used in high-stress areas. Monofilm is light, see-through and extremely stable, but is susceptible to damage and can easily tear if it meets sharp objects. Consequently, sails designed for waves and other more punishing applications will often feature monofilm combined with a lattice of kevlar fibres, which prevents any puncture from spreading too far.

All sails made nowadays, other than children's rigs, incorporate full-length battens. Modern fully battened sails have a 'rotating asymmetric foil' (RAF), whereby the battens slide round the mast to the leeward side of the sail, giving an aerodynamic and efficient shape. Aerodynamic properties can be further enhanced with 'camber-inducers'. These are plastic cupping devices that sit between the batten and the mast, giving an even more wing-like appearance to the leading edge ('luff') of the sail. Camber-inducers greatly increase the stability and speed capabilities of a sail, and are used in all race and slalom sails. However, they make the rig feel stiffer in the hands and less manoeuvrable, so they are not a good choice

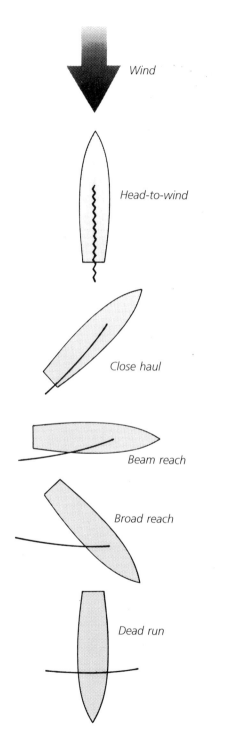

Figure 4 Points of sailing.

for the beginner or for the wave sailor.

Race-oriented sails have six or more battens, most of which will have a camber-inducer fitted for maximum stability and performance. At the other end of the scale, wave or beginner sails will only have four battens for maximum manoeuvrability and ease of use. Four-batten sails are also by far the best choice for sailing in light winds, when stability is not as important as ease of use.

Most sails fall somewhere between these two groups, using almost every possible combination of battens and camber-inducers to cater for any style of recreational sailing. There are also 'variable mode' sails available, whereby camber-inducers and/or battens can be removed or added to increase the sail's stability or manoeuvrability when required.

MASTS Nearly all masts on the market today are made from a fibreglass/carbon composite, with their role and price being determined by the amount of carbon present. Masts intended for recreational use have a carbon content of 10–35 per cent, and weigh around 2.5–3 kg. Performance masts can contain anything from 45–90 per cent carbon, and offer the ultimate in light weight and stiffness.

Masts come with a variety of stiffness values and 'response times', which reflect how quickly the mast can return to its predetermined shape after being bent by a gust. The Indexed Mast Check System (IMCS) is used, featuring a length and stiffness index (e.g. 430 cm, IMCS 25), to detail the performance characteristics of any mast. Sails are usually designed with a particular mast length and stiffness in mind, so referring to the IMCS number will allow you to find the ideal mast for your sail. IMCS values range from around 20 to 35 (20 is the shortest and softest; 30 is the longest and stiffest).

Virtually every mast nowadays comes in two pieces (top half and bottom half), as this makes it much easier to store, whether it is at home, in the car or the cargo hold of a plane.

MAST EXTENSIONS The mast extension is a length of aluminium or carbon tubing (usually between 20 and 45 cm long) that allows different-sized sails to be used with the same mast. It offers adjustment in 5-cm increments through a pin or sliding collar system, and is an essential item for most windsurfers.

This picture shows the difference between a recreational sail (left) and a racing sail (right). Note the extra battens and wide luff sleeve on the racing sail, which provide unparalleled stability, efficiency and power, at the expense of manoeuvrability and ease of use.

Mast lengths range from 400 to 510 cm to accommodate different sizes of sail, but a mast extension allows several sails to be used on the same mast.

The mast extension will usually include the all-important mast foot and 'universal joint', the gadget that allows the rig full freedom of movement and makes windsurfing possible.

BOOMS The boom (Figure 6) is elliptical in shape and consists of two aluminium or carbon tubes coated with a soft rubber grip. These two curved tubes are joined at each end by metal and plastic fittings.

The front-end fitting is critical. A good front end will give a solid mast-to-boom connection, making steering much more positive. For years, booms were simply tied onto the mast with a

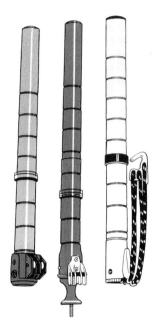

Figure 5 Mast extensions.

Camber-inducer.

piece of rope, and it was quite an achievement to get a reasonably tight connection between the two. Nowadays, booms have a user-friendly, clamp-on front end, ensuring a fast, firm fit. Clamp-on front ends also make it easy to reposition the boom on the mast should it be set too high or low.

The rear boom end should have some form of cleat-and-pulley system for tying off the sail's outhaul. However, it is best not to rely exclusively on the cleats. Always secure the end of the line with a couple of half-hitches.

Most booms are adjustable in body length, so that one boom can be used with a range of sail sizes. The adjustment is achieved either by telescopic or by add-on sections. Most booms adjust in 2.5–5-cm increments, which makes it easy to get the clew of the sail to the desired position near the rear boom end. Telescopic booms use a variety of locking mechanisms, ranging from simple spring-clip collars to complex turn-and-lock systems. However, they are all prone to jamming up with sand and dirt,

and need frequent rinsing in fresh water to maintain their smooth, slide-trombone action.

CHILDREN'S RIGS

To make life easier and more fun for the youngster, specially designed 'kiddy rigs' have been created (Figure 7). Sails on such rigs are small in area, between 2 and 3 m², and usually have no battens at all for lightness and easy uphauling. Masts are very short, very lightweight and small in diameter. The boom is equally small and light, and has much smaller-diameter tubing, making it easier for small hands to grip. A good kiddy rig will feature a large luff cut out in the sail, which leaves plenty of room to raise the boom as the child grows.

WETSUITS

Windsurfing without some form of wetsuit (Figure 8) is not recommended. Apart from the discomfort of getting cold, there is an element

Figure 6 Booms. *(a)* Clamp-on boom end. *(b)* Telescopic and add-on extension booms.

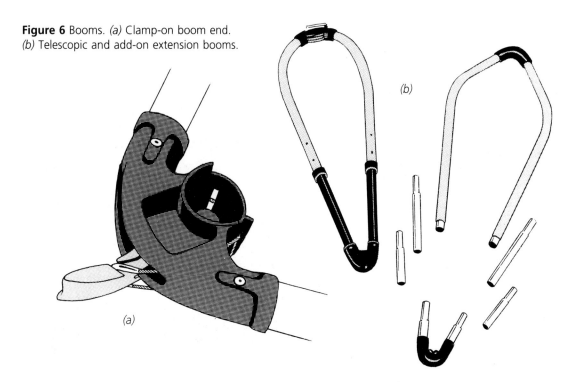

(a)

(b)

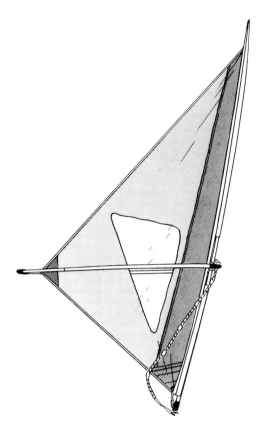

Figure 7 'Kiddy rig', with lightweight, two-part, aluminium mast.

of danger that should not be ignored. The effect of cold water and wind is to reduce the body's core temperature. In extreme cases the chill factor develops into hypothermia, when the sailor can easily slide into unconsciousness and die. A good wetsuit makes it possible to sail even in the coldest of temperatures.

All wetsuits are made from a jigsaw of shaped, neoprene rubber panels. These panels are lined (on one or both sides) with nylon. The single-lined material presents a bare rubber surface to the water, which drips straight off, and is therefore less prone to cause wind chill. Double-lined materials are slightly less slippery, but are harder-wearing.

A wetsuit's thermal qualities depend on the method used to join the rubber panels

together. If they are stitched together using a Mauser or overlock stitch, a lot of water can pass in and out through the holes created. A suit of this type is fine for general use in the summer, but is not suitable for colder conditions. The warmest seam is the blindstitch, which does not penetrate right through the material. If seams are also glued and then taped, they are almost totally watertight. All good winter suits are blindstitched. This is a labour-intensive process, and therefore expensive.

Suits for summer are usually made of rubber 2 or 3 mm thick. The thinness of the material makes these suits easy to overlock, and their inherent flexibility makes them very comfortable to wear. The real icebreaker sailors require 5-mm body suits that are blindstitched. In practice, most suits are of variable thicknesses. Winter suits often have 5-mm body panels, but use 3-mm panels in areas that are flexed a lot, such as the arms and knees.

To work effectively, a wetsuit needs to be a snug fit. A well-fitting suit will trap a thin layer of water, which is then warmed up by body heat. Clearly, a loose-fitting suit that takes in too much water will not have good thermal properties, as every time you take a dip you will

Figure 8 Wetsuits.

get cooled down. Always try a wetsuit on before buying it. Remember that what you need is a well-fitting suit, not a fancy-coloured one!

The style of suit may vary from a simple neoprene vest up to an all-in-one full steamer. Generally, it is better to err on the side of being too warm rather than too cold. Where there are wide seasonal variations in temperature, it makes sense to have a wardrobe of suits for different seasons.

BOOTS, KIDNEY BELTS, HATS AND GLOVES

A good pair of windsurfing shoes or boots is a very wise investment, as the average board has many features to stub the toes on! Shoes or boots also increase grip, and save the feet from shingle, stones and sea urchins. A simple snug-fitting pair of 'surf slippers' is fine for summer. In winter, a pair of thicker neoprene boots that tuck underneath the wetsuit legs (and thus remain dry) is the better option.

Kidney belts or undervests are also useful for keeping warm in colder weather. Some sailors also wear a neoprene balaclava to keep the head warm, although not all sailors like having something over their ears when sailing as it can

affect balance. Gloves are a problem. Although gloves keep the hands warm, they also make it harder to grip the boom, which can soon tire out the forearms. Many sailors prefer to suffer cold fingers in the winter.

HARNESSES

The harness allows sailors to use bodyweight to counter the power in the sail, and dramatically reduces strain on the arms and back. By 'hanging' in the harness, the sailor can also transfer his weight down through the mast into the board, helping hold the nose down when travelling fast and/or in bumpy conditions. Harnesses also allow the use of bigger sails than would otherwise be possible.

A hook at the front of the harness clips over a line attached to the boom at approximately waist level. Without a harness it is impossible to sail for long in strong winds without becoming exhausted. However, harnesses are not much use to beginners, nor to anyone sailing in very light airs. The novice would be well advised to master the basics of windsurfing before thinking about using a harness.

There are three styles of harness available: chest, seat and waist (Figure 9). Seat harnesses are by far the most popular, as the lower hook position gives maximum leverage on the rig. However, some people prefer the feel of a waist harness, particularly those who favour a more upright body stance.

Figure 9 Harnesses. *(a)* Chest. *(b)* Waist. *(c)* Seat.

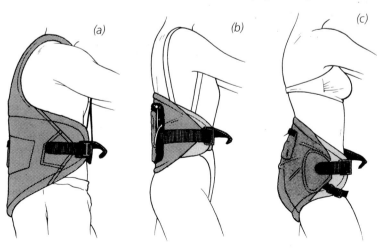

The chest harness is the original form of windsurfing harness. Chest harnesses do not give the same amount of control, and are not so good for the lower back, so they are normally only worn by wave-sailors. A wave-board requires a much more upright style of sailing, for which the chest harness is more appropriate. Chest harnesses also provide an element of upper body protection, which is ideal for the regular crashes and wipe-outs that occur in waves. A chest harness can also offer the most buoyancy of all harnesses, but is still not enough to float an unconscious sailor. Harnesses in general do not provide much flotation, and should not be regarded as buoyancy aids.

ROOF-RACK SYSTEMS

Nearly all windsurfers, unless they live right on the beach, need some sort of transport. If you do not own a van, a roof-rack is an indispensable item of equipment.

Roof-racks come in various shapes and sizes, but usually a traditional Thule or Terzo rack will fit any car with a gutter. These sturdier racks are not cheap, but they do the job best, especially if more than one board needs to be transported. Cars without gutters may be fitted with the appropriate gutterless rack, generally made by the car's manufacturer.

As a rule, the racks should be placed as far apart as possible to spread the load evenly. Boards should be positioned nose forward and fin upwards. If two boards are carried, it is best to stack one on top of the other for maximum aerodynamic efficiency. Be sure to strap the board(s) down securely, using a proper webbing strap with a buckle. Elasticated rope and bits of string will not do, nor for that matter will badly worn straps. Securing valuable equipment with tatty bits of twine may prove to be an expensive and dangerous error.

BOARD INSURANCE

Insuring a board is like insuring a car: third-party liability is essential, safeguarding you should you run into another sailor and inflict injury on him or her and damage his or her equipment. Many beaches and race organizations will not let you sail at their sites if you do not have third-party insurance cover. Comprehensive cover is well worth the additional cost, and you may be pleased you took it if the board is stolen from your car roof. A mechanism to lock board and rig securely to the car roof is advisable, and may be a prerequisite for insurance. Thankfully, board insurance is not too expensive, and there are a number of companies which cater specifically for windsurfers. You will be able to find their advertisements in windsurfing magazines.

3 WINDSURFING COMPETITION

As the sport has evolved, the competitive side has changed many times. Classes and disciplines have appeared, flourished, withered and vanished all in the space of a few years. At the time of writing, competitive windsurfing occurs in two main areas: long-board racing around a course in all wind strengths, and short-board competition in high winds. Long-board racing consists of the International Yacht Racing Union (IYRU) Raceboard class and all One-design classes (including Olympic racing). Short-board competition consists of racing, wave-sailing and speed-sailing disciplines.

LONG-BOARD RACING

RACEBOARD CLASS The Raceboard is a high-volume (usually 250-litre+) long board, designed to be raced in virtually any wind conditions, and usually powered with large (7.5-m^2+) sails. The Raceboard class is managed by the IYRU, and offers extremely competitive racing at all levels. Racing takes place in large combined fleets of often well over 100 sailors, on a course starting with an upwind leg, and then a series of reaches and downwind legs. The beauty of it is that only one board and sail are required for a very wide variety of wind strengths. Raceboards are expensive, of high-tech, lightweight construction, and have a sliding mast track and a very large, fully retractable daggerboard. They are the fastest thing on the water in non-planing conditions, particularly upwind. This type of board is also used in a wide range of other 'one-off' style events, such as marathons, long-distance events and round-island races.

ONE-DESIGN CLASSES A couple of long boards have also been designated official 'one-design' (OD) racing boards, whereby everyone in the race fleet is competing on the same equipment.

This means that the boards used do not have to be specifically designed for racing, so can be cheaper, more durable and easier to sail than a specialist racing design.

The longest standing OD class in the world is the Windsurfer Regatta, a board that first appeared in 1976. The board remains approximately the same shape and build as the original Windsurfer, but the rig has been improved in line with modern sail technology. Another very durable and inexpensive OD class uses the Tiga Aloha 365, which has been adopted as the official international youth class. Up-and-coming stars cut their teeth in this fleet, and consequently it offers some of the most hotly contested racing available.

Olympic (IMCO) Class Racing This is the one-design class chosen for the 1996 Olympics. Mistral have been running a successful OD class for many years, but use a much more race-oriented design than other OD classes.

Although the board is now a few years old and somewhat heavier (and cheaper!) than modern raceboards, it can still give modern raceboards a run for their money in the hands of top racers. The board used for International Mistral Class Organization (IMCO) racing has changed a few times over the years, and the 7.5-m^2 sail has been updated. It is now a sophisticated racing sail, and both the down-haul and outhaul can be adjusted by the sailor while racing.

IMCO racing has always been popular, with well-attended national, European and World championships. Now that it is the official Olympic board, IMCO has attracted all the best sailors from the Raceboard class, and the standard is unequalled. The usual Olympic course is the 'box' course. This involves all points of sailing, starting on a beat (traditionally the leg where most ground is won or lost), moving onto a close reach, and then a run, for a number of laps.

Like the Raceboard and all other OD classes, Olympic racing can happen in non-planing conditions, during which sail-pumping for extra speed is allowed. As a race can last for up to half an hour, the Olympic class is not just about skill and tactics. There is also an immense requirement for fitness and stamina.

LONG-BOARD FREESTYLE The only other form of long-board competition is freestyle, where sailors show off their board- and sail-handling skills in a carefully choreographed tricks routine to impress the judges. Competition is usually man-on-man (where two or more sailors perform at the same time and winners are picked by a panel of judges), but there are other variations.

High-wind wave-sailing in big surf is definitely for experts only.

Freestyle was once extremely popular, but lost popularity with the rise of funboarding and stronger-wind sailing. Nevertheless, it remains an ideal fun activity in light winds, and is a great way of perfecting board-handling skills.

SHORT-BOARD RACING

FUNBOARD RACING This occurs in planing conditions only. Consequently it is fast, exciting, and often happens in trickier sea states, giving a lot more to worry about than pure racing tactics.

The top funboard class circuit is the Professional Windsurfers Association (PWA) World Tour, in which competitors who have been successful at national level can turn professional and participate on the international circuit.

The start of an IMCO Class race, with everyone racing on the same Olympic Class board.

Slalom racers blasting towards the gybe mark.

The World Tour consists of about 30 prize-money events, and the standard of sailing is as high as it gets, as these sailors are doing it for a living. However, with the cost of extra-specialized equipment and the expense of globe-trotting to far-flung locations, competing on the World Tour is a pastime for the favoured few. It is a very difficult circuit for the newcomer to break into.

Fortunately for the would-be funboard racer, there is also plenty of competition at lower levels. The International Funboard Class Association (IFCA) oversees active and well-subscribed racing associations in most countries. In the UK, the British Windsurfing Association (BWA) organizes events around the year, at coastal locations where conditions are known to be good.

At every level other than the World Cup, funboard racing is normally conducted on 'production kit', that is equipment that can be bought from a retailer. Most brands have very raceworthy equipment in their range for this purpose. IFCA have European and World production funboard championships, and there is a lot of prestige at stake for the brand that wins. Some countries allow sailors to race on custom equipment as preparation for the World Cup circuit, but racers who compete on custom boards are not eligible for the production board international regattas.

Nowadays, funboard racing is totally dominated by short boards. The most modern 'Marginal Wind Raceboard' designs (usually 280–295 cm) can plane in as little as 8 knots of breeze, so this is the present minimum wind requirement for funboard racing. In these winds, races are usually set around a course involving some upwind work, although the course itself is totally at the discretion of the race officer. Either the whole fleet races as one, or it is split into two or more groups that race around the course separately, and the leading sailors go on to a group final.

If the wind is over 15 knots, then funboard racing can be based on a slalom format (Figure 10). This is where top speed skills and perfect gybing performance are required. Sailors select

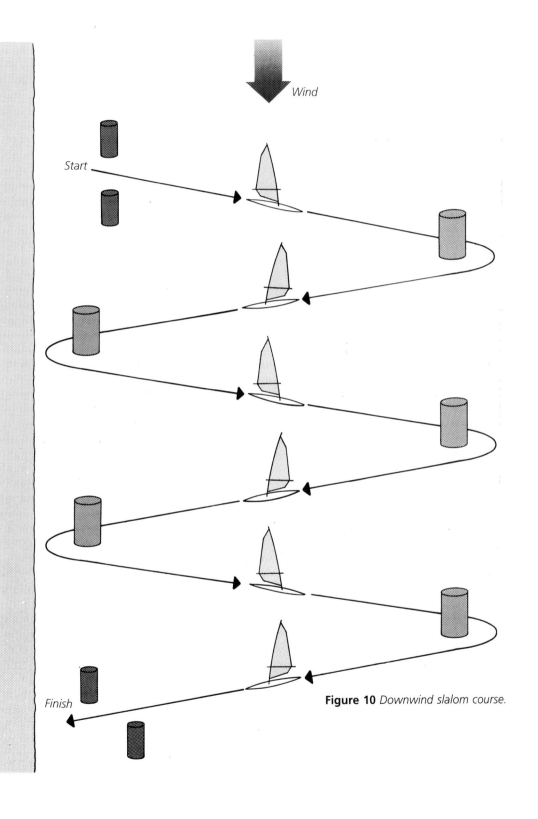

Figure 10 *Downwind slalom course.*

their shorter boards (usually 275 cm or smaller), and race in heats of eight or ten around a two-buoy, figure-of-eight course. Slalom is also run on a downwind slalom course around four, five or even six gybes to a finish line maybe a kilometre downwind of the start. This type of course makes it much easier for spectators to watch the action.

Slalom races begin either with a 'Le Mans' start from the beach, or with a 'line-start' out to sea. In a line-start, sailors jockey for position during the countdown, and try to time their run-up to cross the line at full speed, exactly as the green flag goes up. The start is often the most important part of the race. One second early and you are disqualified; one second late and you are at the back of the fleet in dirty wind and water.

Slalom competition is usually based on a knockout format, where the top three or four sailors from each round go on to the next round. First-round heats progress to quarter-finals, semi-finals and then the final itself. Slalom racing is high-speed and spectacular, often with big wipe-outs at the corners. It is also an easy form of racing to organize. Two buoys are all that are required, and with starts going from the beach it is possible to run races in the most crazy conditions. Slalom is often run on a very informal basis, where a few sailors get together and organize their own races around mooring buoys or crab-pots. Any slalom-style board can be used for competition at this level.

WAVE-SAILING COMPETITIONS Wave-riding and jumping is short-board sailing at its most exciting, both for the competitor and spectator. Wave competition sees sailors pushing themselves and their kit to the maximum in the allotted time, to impress the panel of judges ashore.

Competition wave-riding began in Hawaii, but has since been adopted in many other countries. Although wave-sailing action can be spectacular in anything from cross-offshore to directly onshore winds, ideally a wave contest

Table-top jump.

should be held in cross-shore conditions. This allows the sailor to perform the greatest variety of manoeuvres both coming in and going out through the surf. A minimum wind of around 8–10 knots is usually required, though in such light winds it is difficult to get planing, and the action is likely to be wave-riding only. The stronger the wind the more spectacular the action, as the faster the sailors can go the higher they can jump.

Wave contests happen all over the world, but the number one site is without question Ho'okipa Beach Park in Maui, Hawaii. This is a natural amphitheatre site with big waves and regular trade winds, used for the most prestigious contests and as a training/proving ground for all the world's best wave-sailors.

The nature of competitive wave-riding clearly differs from racing, and placing the sailors in order of merit is a matter of judgement. Judges base their decision on three categories: jumping, riding and transitions. A time limit is set, bearing in mind the prevailing conditions. Heats are usually of between five and ten minutes' duration. The most common scoring format is that the best three jumps, rides and transitions count, but how much emphasis is placed on each category depends on the conditions. Sometimes wave-riding is scored most highly, while in more cross-onshore conditions (when wave-riding is more difficult and less visually impressive) jumping may earn more points. Including a variety of manoeuvres in the programme makes a good impression. Equally, repetition of the same manoeuvre, no matter how well you do it, will quickly pall.

Wave-riding is scored on the length and quality of ride, along with initial wave selection. A wave-ride can last for some time, and points are gained for the number and quality of bottom turns and top turns, aerials, re-entries etc. Nowadays, radical aerial moves performed while wave-riding, such as the gu-screw, 360 and goiter, score most highly.

The variety of extremely radical and dangerous aerial manoeuvres now being pulled off means that the basic jump, no matter how high, will not be scored very highly in a wave contest, especially at top level. Even a single forward loop will not impress the judges very

Wave-riding.

much. Until recently it was vital to complete the manoeuvre to score any points at all, which meant that sailors tended to 'sail safe', rather than trying anything extreme. Now the rules have been relaxed slightly to allow sailors to 'go for it' more.

Finally, good transitions on the outside and inside can sway a decision. Difficult transitions, like aerial gybes, duck gybes and duck tacks all score points, but must be completed with dry hair!

SPEED-SAILING COMPETITIONS This is undoubtedly the most popular 'unofficial' discipline in the sport, as windsurfers seem to spend most of their time trying to sail faster than each other. Windsurfers can travel very fast indeed, and are the fastest standard production water-craft by far. Most modern small slalom boards can achieve speeds of around 40 knots (about 80 kph) or more.

Competitive speed sailing used to be simple – the fastest sailor between two points won. However, this meant that competitors were not motivated to try their hardest on lighter wind days of the competition, when speeds were unlikely to be very high anyway.

Forward loop sequence. Once airborne, the sailor sheets in and throws the board forward into the loop to rotate fully through 360°. Sheeting in or out will vary the speed of rotation, so the sailor can adjust his or her sheeting angle to land back in the sailing position and – hopefully – not even get wet.

Today, most official speed events are run as a series of separate 'legs', and the overall winner is the sailor who has most consistently sailed fast throughout the event. This system encourages sailors to do their best whatever the weather. The highest-ranked speed-sailors in the world are those who can sail fast in a wide range of conditions, so the world speed record-holder might not necessarily be the world champion speed-sailor.

Speed-sailing at national and international level seems to attract a specific breed of sailor. To be a top-class speed-sailor, you need to be very big, very strong and very aggressive. All the fastest men in the world are well over 90 kg, which helps them to control the big sails used, often in ridiculously strong winds. Size has not been quite so important in the women's fleet, but the need for strength and aggression is still definitely there, as is the need to be tough. Speed-sailing can be extremely painful. The water feels like concrete if you 'wipe out' at 65 kph, and injuries are common at top level.

Originally, everyone competed on specialist custom-built speed equipment. Today, the speed difference between specialist speed boards and modern production small slalom boards is so little (barely a knot) that many sailors choose to compete on production equipment. The same goes for sails. Speed-sailing requires maximum stability and aerodynamic efficiency from a rig, which is exactly what racing sails are about. There are no specialist speed-sails currently in production.

The ideal speed-sailing location requires strong, constant winds blowing at the right direction, and very flat water. Boards built for speed are low in volume and very narrow, in order to minimize the amount of underside area in contact with the water. They need winds well above Force 4 simply to get going. The wind needs to be not only strong but also constant in nature, undisturbed by buildings, trees or similar objects that might interfere with its free flow. Ideally, the speed-sailor wants to be fully powered up for the entire length of the run. Water conditions are also very important. In order for a sailor to go fast and maintain any form of control, the water must be as flat as possible.

Start buoy

Wind

Figure 11 Speed course.

On top of this, the wind has to blow from exactly the right direction, so that boards can be sailed at 110–130° to the wind in the flattest water available. With all these requirements, suitable top-class locations for speed-sailing are difficult to find. The main problem is that where it is very windy the water is generally not flat. Sotavento, on the Canary island of Fuerteventura, is a favoured location, as the prevailing wind blows directly offshore, making the water close to the beach reasonably smooth. Tarifa in southern Spain also offers these conditions, along with exceptionally strong thermal winds in the summer months.

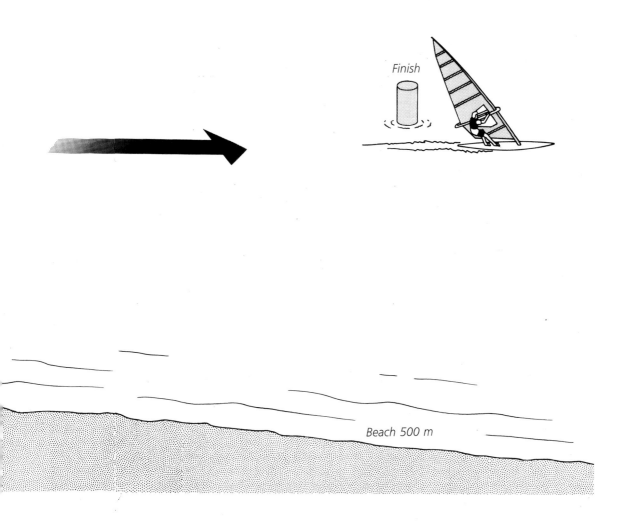

The present open-sea speed record was set at Tarifa. In the UK, the most popular location is the lake at West Kirby in Wirral, where the low harbour wall is ideally angled to the prevailing wind and provides smooth water conditions. Another location becoming increasingly popular is 'The Ray' at Southend-on-Sea, where a small channel is uncovered between the mudflats at low tide.

Other sites are being discovered, but the lack of world-class speed-sailing locations has led to manmade courses being constructed, at considerable expense. A purpose-built canal or 'ditch' was dug at St Marie in the south of France. Regular open and 'private' competitions are held there, and often a top speed-sailor will hire the ditch in a personal attempt to break the world record.

Speed-sailing at top level is a very specialist discipline for a few hardy souls. However, everyone likes to know how fast they are going, so less formal speed events often occur. Many of these are run over a shorter (100-m) course, or perhaps simply using a police-style radar 'speed gun'. Many national speed-sailing authorities have video and computer-timing facilities that can be lent or hired to clubs wishing to run their own event.

4 RULES AND SAFETY

One of the main attractions of recreational windsurfing is that it is a 'free' activity, unencumbered by rules and regulations. Nevertheless, there are occasions when common sense, rather than a rigid set of rules, comes into play.

Collisions are to be avoided at all costs. Boards and sails are easily damaged in this way, to say nothing of the potential for personal injury. The risk of collision is always there, no matter how good you are, as people tend to windsurf towards the limits of their control skills. Beginners are obviously less able to control their board's direction and/or take rapid avoiding action, while more experienced sailors are usually travelling a lot faster. So, whatever your ability, always keep a good lookout ahead, and check behind you before tacking or gybing as this is a very common cause of conflict. Get into the habit of cultivating spatial awareness. Note the whereabouts of other sailors, and the location of obstacles such as buoys or rocks.

As a rule, the windsurfer should give way to any object considered less manoeuvrable. Surfers, canoeists and, most importantly, swimmers fall into this category. Any powered craft, on the other hand, should give way to the windsurfer. This includes jetskis, launches and motorboats of any description. Do not assume that because you have seen the powered vessel its captain has seen you. Although the official rule is 'steam gives way to sail', there is also the practical consideration of 'might has right'. Big craft, in particular tankers, coasters, warships and ferries, are simply not able to manoeuvre very quickly. The best advice is always to keep clear.

As for other windsurfers and sailing craft, the basic 'port and starboard' rule applies (Figure

The smile says it all!

12). If sailors are on opposite tacks, the sailor on starboard tack has right of way, and the port-tack sailor must stay clear. Remember that when your right hand is nearest the mast you are on starboard tack, and if it is the left hand you are on port tack. If both sailors are on the same tack, then the craft running free should give way. The sailor on a broad reach should give way to a sailor to windward who is on a tighter heading.

RACING RULES

When racing, knowledge of the rules is crucial, as even the best sailor can lose on a technicality. Many original International Yacht Racing Union (IYRU) rules have had to be modified to suit windsurfing. Racing can involve some very complicated situations, and many problems have to be sorted out in the Protest Room. Here, a complaint is heard by a jury of skilled racers, with witnesses called and statements taken.

The rule most invoked is number 36, regarding port and starboard priority. In a race situation a cry of 'starboard' means that the sailor on port tack is obliged to give way. Another general rule is that the windward craft must keep clear of the leeward craft. This rule is very useful on a reach or sailing upwind, as it is very difficult to overtake someone unless you sail past them to windward. They can make life as difficult as possible by sailing closer and closer to the wind ('luffing' you). You must keep clear until you have established a true overlap with the board you are trying to overtake, whereupon you can shout 'MAST ABEAM!', and they must bear off to let you past.

Rules for overtaking at the mark are complex, and the situation is often very confused because it is the most common place for people to fall

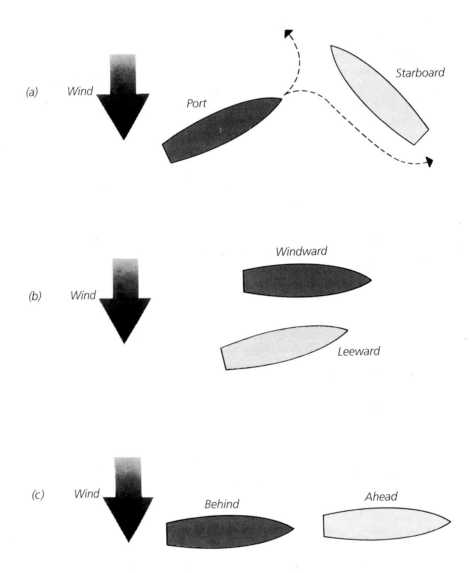

Figure 12 Rights of way –
in each case the lighter-shaded board has right of way.
(a) Port board keeps clear of starboard.
(b) Windward board keeps clear of leeward.
(c) Board behind keeps clear of another ahead.

in. With some sailors in the water, and others jostling for the best position after the turn, there is much opportunity for conflict. However, unlike dinghy and yacht racing, windsurfers are usually allowed to touch the mark, which makes life easier.

The port/starboard and windward rules also apply at the start, so it is important not to get caught out at this critical stage. With the first leg of the course being usually directly upwind, you can start on either tack. Usually, the advantage is with those on starboard, unless the line has been set with a very large 'port bias', to favour those wishing to try a 'port flyer' start.

Slalom racing is not as complicated. There are fewer sailors involved, the course is simple, and everyone starts on the same reaching tack. The main rules to worry about concern port/starboard and overtaking. Normally, if you are over the line at the start, you are disqualified immediately. This prevents sailors trying to turn back into oncoming traffic in an attempt to recross the line properly.

SURF-SAILING

IYRU rules do not apply in surf locations. Even rules regarding port and starboard are largely ignored. There is a common consensus, though, that the sailor going out through the waves has right of way over the sailor coming in. This makes sense, because the incoming rider has more control and ability to change direction.

If there are two or more sailors on the same wave, then the one who is furthest upwind has control. Should he or she decide to ride downwind, then other sailors must respect this decision and keep clear.

It is not good form to make a transition onto a wave purely to gain the upwind position. If the wave has already formed, and a sailor gybes onto it upwind of others, he has no rights. In a roundabout way this leads on to another rule: the sailor who catches the wave first has priority. A sailor cannot come onto the wave from behind and expect any water.

Finally, the sailor nearest the most critical part of the wave (the part just about to break) has priority. This rule gives a sailor who is trying to work the most powerful part of the wave

freedom to do so. Often novice wave-sailors do not use the full power of the wave, and ride the shallower and more forgiving sections. The experts have no problem with that, as long as they are also allowed to get to the part of the wave they want to ride.

SAFETY

Equipment failure is a serious matter, so always check your gear before going on the water. Lines are very susceptible to wear, so make a careful check and replace worn ones. The universal joint (UJ) is also subject to a great deal of wear and tear, so it is a good idea to have a 'UJ saver' fitted. This webbing reinforcement means that even if the universal joint snaps far offshore you can still get back.

Try not to sail for extended periods without a break. It is easy to become tired, especially if you have not mastered using a harness. If you drift downwind, you may find that you are too exhausted to sail back upwind to your original launch site.

Lastly, take note of weather conditions before you go out. Always check the weather report as a matter of course, and be aware that weather conditions can change rapidly. Tell someone where you intend to be sailing, and how long you expect to be gone. Unless very experienced, never sail in an offshore wind. Many novices venture out in conditions way beyond their capabilities. If in doubt, do not go out! Do not be afraid to ask fellow sailors for advice about the best sail size to use, or about tides and currents. Knowledge of local conditions is an indispensable asset to any sailor, and not just the windsurfer.

Should you get into difficulties, try to attract the attention of another sailor who can give you a tow to safety. Since voices do not carry very well on a windy day at sea, make your intentions clear by using the international distress signal (Figure 13). Sit astride your board and move both arms up and down in a flying action. If someone spots you they should come to your assistance.

If the situation is not desperate, and you are close to the shore, a self-rescue may be feasible, but do not embark on this operation

Figure 13 This up-and-down motion of the arms, sitting astride the board, is a universally recognized distress signal.

and then change your mind halfway through. Knowledge of self-rescue technique is essential for anyone who puts out to sea – or indeed inland waters – on a board.

In the 'old days', self-rescue was a simple matter of removing all the battens and rolling the sail around the mast. Modern sail design makes that much more difficult, if not impossible, so before derigging the sail consider other options carefully.

Many broken components (including fins) are a nuisance, but do not necessarily render the board unsailable. If the UJ has snapped, ask a passing sailor to put your rig inside his and sail it ashore, while you paddle your board home. However, if you have broken your mast, then you will have to derig and pack everything up onto the board. Tie everything together with downhaul rope, uphauls, outhauls, and harness lines so you can lie on top of it all and paddle home. A useful tip when derigging the sail is to wedge a section of the mast through the back footstraps on your board. This will make the board much more stable, but be sure to remove it when you start paddling, as it creates drag.

If you are in a very tight situation, or cannot make headway, do not be afraid to ditch the rig and paddle the hull ashore. The golden rule is that, whatever the circumstances and no matter how well you can swim, DO NOT leave the board and make a break for it. The buoyancy of the board is definitely your best friend at this time.

5 Technique

There have been literally millions of words written on windsurfing technique. All the leading magazines run regular technique articles, addressing every level of the sport from beginner to expert.

While there are many sports that are more difficult and demanding than windsurfing, it is nevertheless fairly technical, and requires application, persistence and patience. Unlike other dynamic sports such as skiing, snow-boarding, skateboarding, mountain-biking and many others, the windsurfing environment is constantly changing. You can never go back and repeat a manoeuvre exactly as before. If the wind strength or direction has not changed, then the water surface certainly will have. Indeed, trying to learn new windsurfing tech-niques in gusty, choppy conditions can be incredibly frustrating, and generally is not recommended.

BEGINNERS' TECHNIQUES

Anyone of any age with reasonable balance and coordination can learn to windsurf. Naturally, it is not just a matter of getting on the board and sailing away. Inevitably you will flounder and struggle for a while, but the learning process can be shortened if the steps involved are analysed and understood beforehand. Without question, the best way to learn is to be taught, rather than trying to work it all out for yourself or relying on a friend. This means going to a Royal Yachting Association (RYA) recognized windsurfing school run by professionals.

If there is no RYA school nearby, or you are simply determined to have a go at it alone, then this is how you get started.

RIGGING-UP Setting up the rig is a simple process, and generally takes around 10–15 minutes if done methodically. It is a mistake to try to rig up in too much of a hurry. A poorly rigged sail will only have to be rigged again after a spell of unsatisfactory sailing.

Unless brand new, your sail should have the battens in place already. Slide the mast up the sail's luff sleeve until the mast tip is nestling firmly into the sail's head cap. (If the mast is reluctant to slide up the luff sleeve, detension the battens slightly.) Insert the mast foot or mast extension into the mast base, and either thread the downhaul rope into the tack pulley-and-cleat system, or hook the pulley hook into the eyelet, depending on what system your sail uses. If the sail has an adjustable head, it will need to be set to the correct length, so that when the sail is downhauled properly the tack eyelet is as close to the mast-foot pulley block and cleat as possible.

Attach the boom securely to the mast anywhere from chest to shoulder height, depending on where you want it. Most people go for somewhere in between. Now go to the rear boom end, or outhaul. Modern sails set almost entirely on downhaul tension, so for the moment just outhaul the sail roughly to its known boom length, using any integral rear boom pulleys if you have them. Now go back to the downhaul for a good hard pull. Most modern sails require a lot of downhaul tension. Pulleys on the mast foot or mast extension are essential to gain a 4:1, 6:1 or even 8:1 ratio. To save your hands from rope burn, use a down-hauling device. Known variously as 'grunts', 'rig pullas', or 'easy rigs', these indispensable items of kit offer a pain-free method of exerting downhaul pressure. To make tensioning easier, sit down, and with bent knees, place one foot on the base of the mast foot. The best technique is to push simultaneously with your foot and leg while pulling the line, keeping the back as straight as possible.

Knowing how much downhaul tension to

This is the best way to apply downhaul tension, but you may prefer to wear shoes if you value your feet.

apply is something that comes with experience. However, it is difficult to over-downhaul a modern sail, so do not be afraid to apply plenty of tension.

When enough downhaul tension has been applied, return to the outhaul and adjust if necessary so that the sail does not touch the boom sides when it is filled with wind. If you detensioned the battens to sleeve the mast, now is the time to reapply tension so that any vertical wrinkles along the batten pockets disappear.

Small adjustments to downhaul and outhaul tension can greatly affect how the sail performs, so it is important to have it tuned correctly for the conditions. The most common error is insufficient downhaul tension. A sail that is correctly downhauled can actually look a mess on the beach, since the head and upper leech appear far too floppy and creased. However, once on the water this upper area of the sail will tighten up to perfection under load from the wind.

Derigging is simply a reversal of the rigging-up procedure.

CARRYING BOARD AND RIG Long boards are cumbersome to carry to the water's edge. Hold the board on its side, using the daggerboard slot or mast track as a firm place to grip and balance it roughly about its central point. For those of slighter build and/or in more windy conditions, it is best to carry the board between two people. Always take the board first and then return for the rig. An untethered rig left lying around in the wind can easily blow away.

At first you will get blown all over the place when you try to carry the rig, but as you learn to let the wind help you it becomes effortless. Always stand to windward (back to wind) of the

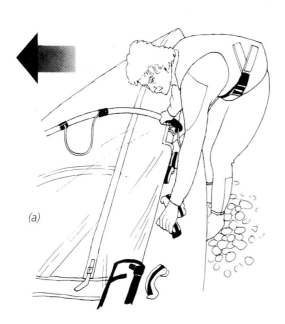

Figure 14 Carrying the board as one unit. *(a)* Lay the board across the rig and approach from the upwind side. *(b)* Lift the board with the front footstrap and the top of the boom, so that the wind blows under the hull and sail.

rig with the mast nearest to you. Have the foot of the sail pointing in the direction you intend to travel. The rig should then be easy to lift with one hand on the mast and the other on the boom, whereupon the wind will flow under the sail, making it lighter. The golden rule with windsurfing is to make the wind do the work for you.

Shorter and lighter boards can be transported with the rig attached (Figure 14). Start with the board positioned across the wind and the rig downwind, with the mast lying towards the back of the board. Position yourself between the tail of the board and the rig, and lift the whole lot together, holding one of the windward footstraps and the boom. As you lift the board, the wind should blow under the hull and rig, helping you on your way.

As you progress onto smaller boards, transportation problems become easier. Waveboards and their rigs can be carried on top of the head (this is not recommended with bigger boards if you value your spine).

UPHAULING Place the board in the water at 90° to the wind, allowing enough depth so that when you fall off you do not hit the bottom too hard. To get aboard, approach the hull from the windward side, making sure that the sail is downwind of the board. Climb up onto the board near the mast-foot area, which is usually the most buoyant and stable part. Kneel down astride the mast foot to get better balance (Figure 15).

If you take the uphaul rope with the front hand it will act as a counterweight against which you can lean to help your balance. Using the uphaul as an aid, straighten yourself up gradually, keeping your knees bent and back straight. This will lower your centre of gravity and improve your balance. Place your feet about shoulder-width apart either side of the mast foot. By holding the uphaul you can keep the rig at approximately 90° to the hull by exerting left- and right-foot pressure.

To lift the sail, straighten your legs and back while pulling the uphaul (Figure 16). Initially, this will be difficult because of the weight of water lying on the sail. As the water drains off,

Figure 15 Uphauling. *(a)* Kneel astride the mast foot. *(b)* Holding the uphaul with your front hand, straighten up gradually. *(c)* Lift the sail by straightening your legs and back while pulling the uphaul.

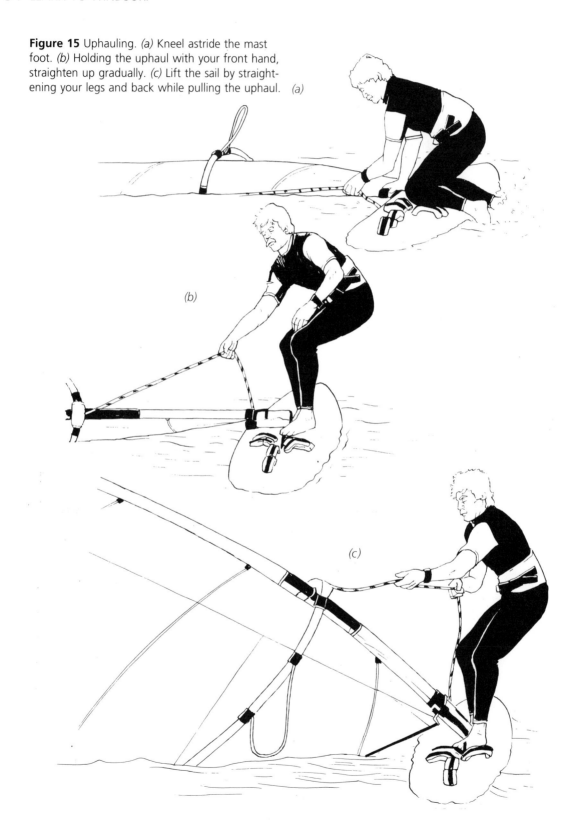

Figure 16 The start position.

continue straightening your legs while taking in the uphaul with a hand-over-hand motion. It gets easier as water drains off the sail and out of the luff tube. (Learners often forget to anticipate this, and pull too hard for too long. The result is a back flop into the water, quickly followed by the sail.) Once you have got the sail out of the water, let it flap freely in the breeze, so it is blowing directly downwind. This gives you an important indication of wind direction.

Transfer one or both hands to hold the mast below the boom. This is a relaxed and stable position that you can return to in any moment of doubt, and should be thought of as a neutral, secure position (Figure 17), balanced and ready for action, but not yet moving forward.

SAILING AWAY Having mastered the secure position, it is now time for some forward motion and the transition to the sailing position (Figure 18). Keeping the mast in its original plane, move both feet back. Your front foot should be next to the mast foot and pointing forward, and your rear foot a comfortable stride further back, somewhere adjacent to the

Figure 17 The secure position.

Figure 18 The sailing position.

daggerboard casing. This is the start position. Turn to face your direction of travel, and swivel the hips in that direction. Then pull the rig to a balance point to windward, near to your front shoulder. At the balance point the rig should feel almost weightless.

In one movement, place your rear hand (the 'sheeting' hand) on the boom. The sail will immediately start to power up, and the board will move forward. When it feels comfortable, place your front hand near the front of the boom. Relocate your body weight onto the rear foot to counterbalance any pull from the rig. You should now be comfortable and moving forward in the recognized 'sailing position'.

BASIC STEERING With a little practice it does not take long to feel comfortable and at ease in the sailing position. The next priority is steering, either up towards the wind, which is called 'heading up' (Figure 19), or turning the

Figure 19 Heading up (*turning the board into the eye of the wind*). Tilt the rig backwards and sheet in with your sail hand. As the pressure on the sail increases, move your rear foot back to help balance. When you are pointing in the right direction, tilt the rig forward again.

nose of the board further away from the wind, known as 'bearing away' (Figure 20). Heading up is the easier of the two manoeuvres. From the sailing position, on a reach, you start to head up by tilting the rig aft. As you do so, sheet in harder with the back hand and move your weight aft to aid the turn. The nose of the board will head up towards the wind. To stop the turning movement, simply tilt the mast back towards its original position.

To start bearing away, tilt the mast forward (quite far, if the wind is not too strong) and again sheet in. Once the board starts to react, sheet out a touch and reposition your weight forward. When you are heading in your intended direction, again tilt the mast back to its original position to sail in a straight line.

TURNING AROUND To get back to the point where you started, you need to turn the board around. This can either be done by a 180° upwind turn, known as a tack, or a 180° downwind turn, known as a gybe. Tacking is the easier of the two, but for the more competent sailor the gybe is generally the more exciting and spectacular way of turning the board.

Tacking The most basic tack is initiated from the secure position (Figure 21). Tilt the mast towards the board's tail to make the nose turn towards the eye of the wind. Keep leaning the rig aft until the board is head-to-wind. Take little steps throughout so you are always facing the mast, with one foot each side of – and very close to – the mast foot. Continue to tilt the mast and rig back until the board has spun a complete 180°. Assume a new, secure position on the new tack.

Once the basic idea is grasped, you can

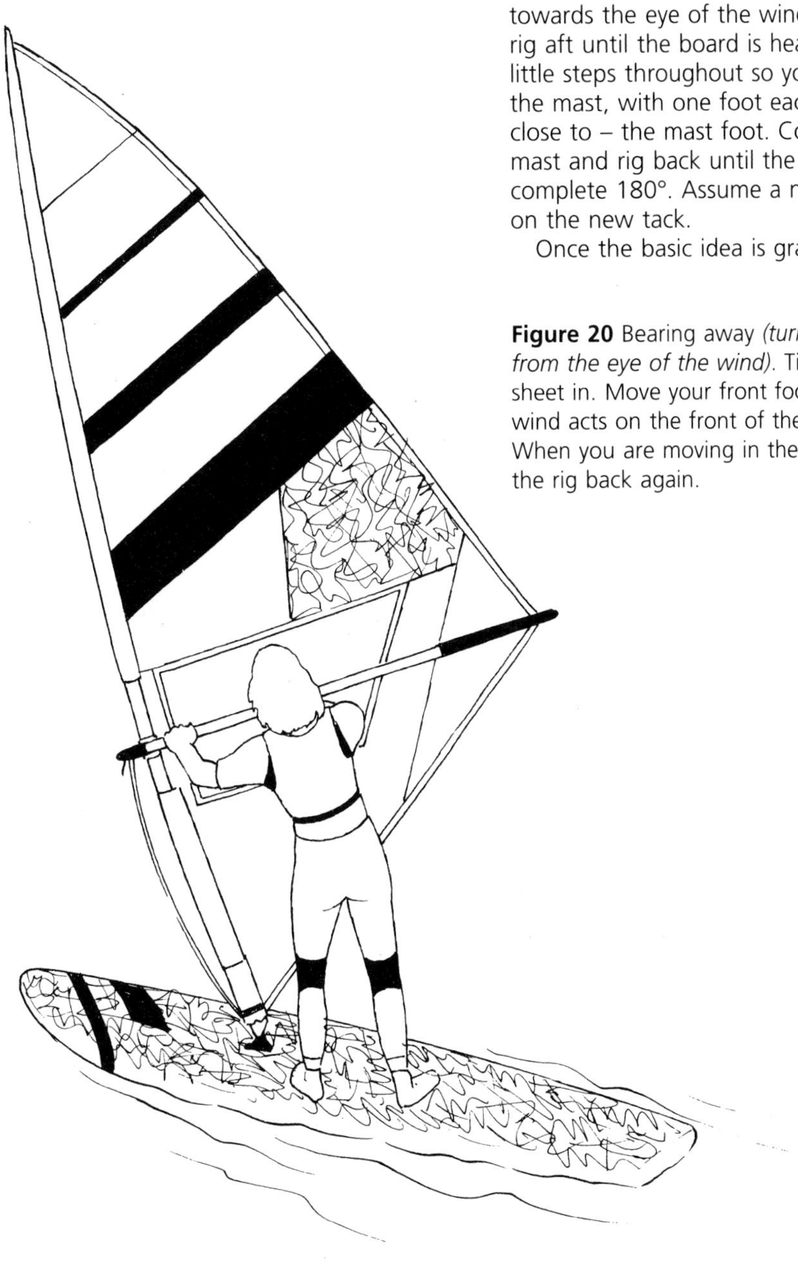

Figure 20 Bearing away *(turning the board away from the eye of the wind)*. Tilt the rig forward and sheet in. Move your front foot forwards as the wind acts on the front of the sail and sheet out. When you are moving in the right direction, tilt the rig back again.

Figure 21 Tacking. *(a)* Approach with enough momentum to get you through the turn. Begin to lean back and sheet in slightly. *(b)* Transfer your front foot to just in front of the mast and your front hand to the mast below the boom. Keep the rig angled back. *(c)* When the board slows down and turns head to wind (or preferably just after), bring your back foot up to join your front foot, and your back hand up to join your front hand on the mast. *(d)* Reach for the boom with what was your front hand and bring the sail across your body and sheet in. *(e)* Sail away on the new tack.

speed up the tacking process. The harder you sheet in, and the further you position your weight aft, the faster the turn. From a sailing position you can hop round the mast and, with good timing, immediately take the new boom to bear away in a new sailing position. On shorter boards, the quick tack or 'jump tack' is the only way to tack the board, since if you spend any more time standing in front of the mast foot the nose will sink completely.

Gybing From a sailing position, tilt the mast forward and slightly to windward by extending the leading arm as for bearing away (Figure 22). As the nose of the board turns away from the wind, continue this steering motion, sheeting out a little as you point further downwind. As you approach a dead downwind point of

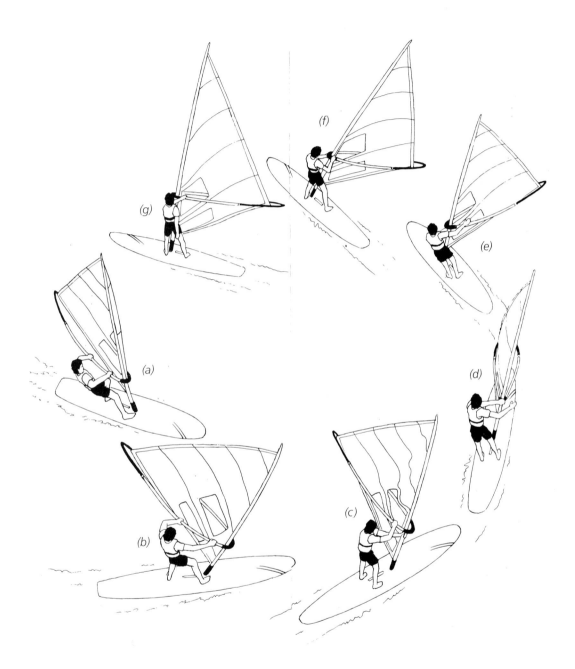

Figure 22 Basic gybing. *(a)* From a beam reach, bear away. *(b)* Sheet in a little with the sail hand. *(c)* Tilt the mast sideways so that the board turns out of the wind. Position feet either side of the daggerboard casing. Grasp the mast with your rear hand. *(d)* You are now on a run. Grasp the boom front (or the uphaul). *(e)* The sail swings round over the bow. *(f)* Lean the sail into the wind. *(g)* Tilt the mast forward and sheet in.

sailing, known as a run, move your front foot aft to stand on either side of the board's centreline near the daggerboard casing.

To continue the turn and gybe the sail, take your rear hand from the boom to grasp the mast. With the help of the wind, swing the sail over the nose of the board. For the first few attempts it is a good idea to reassume the start position before setting off on the new tack.

It should not take the enthusiastic learner too long to master the basic gybe. However, it will always be a rather wobbly and uncertain move, and there are a variety of more advanced gybing techniques to speed up the turn and decrease the turning circle required.

In the 'flare gybe', the rig operation is very similar in motion to the standard gybe, but more exaggerated in effect. To turn tightly, push the daggerboard down fully. Get well back on the board, and from a reach depress the windward rail, whereupon the board will spin on its axis. The flare gybe requires better balance and timing than the conventional long-board gybe.

INTERMEDIATE TECHNIQUES

Once these basic steering and turning techniques have been mastered, the door is open for plenty of easy and enjoyable sailing on any relatively floaty and stable board, in winds of up to 10–12 knots. For windsurfing in these winds, you do not need to learn anything more, but there are plenty of techniques that will definitely make life easier, and allow you to sail for longer.

THE BEACH-START The windsurfer who has mastered the art of beach-starting has a distinct advantage over the windsurfer who can only uphaul. Uphauling can be a tedious and exhausting business, especially in high winds and rough water. Not only is the beach-start more convenient but it is also much more stylish.

Ideally, a Force 2–3 wind is required for first attempts at beach-starting (Figure 23). Make sure the daggerboard is retracted, so that the board can manoeuvre more freely about the fin. Position the board in the shallows, about knee-deep, directly across the wind. Standing to windward of the board, hold the boom in the sailing position. Use mast-foot pressure to maintain the board's position. Pushing down through the mast foot will bear the board away, whereas pulling up through the mast foot will make the board luff up.

Raise the rig slightly so you can get nearer to the board close to the footstraps. Place your back foot on the board, directly on its centre-line. To generate lift, bear away and extend your front arm to present the sail to the wind. Control any undue pull from the sail by sheeting in or out with the back hand. As you extend both arms, hop aboard with your front foot. If you time this movement to coincide with a gust, the wind will do even more of the work for you.

Once safely aboard, move the sail straight into the sailing position, and if necessary get your weight forward very quickly to stop the board heading into the wind. Of course, the long-board beach start is readily adaptable to short-board sailing once you progress that far.

STANCE An efficient stance is the key to good windsurfing technique, and maximizes enjoyment while minimizing effort. The classic windsurfing stance is the upturned 'A' position. The sailor (with legs and back fairly straight) leans back against the rig, which is also leaning out, and the arms are straight and horizontal, giving the crossbar of the 'A'. Both hands should be positioned at an equal distance from the rig's balance point. Shoulder-width apart is about right. How you grip the boom is a matter of personal choice. The leading-hand grip can be either overhand or underhand, but the back-hand grip should certainly be overhand. Use your lower torso as a counterbalance against gusts to keep the rig upright. When the wind drops and lulls occur, shift your hips in and upwards. In the gusts, move them out to take the strain of extra pull from the rig. Your legs should be slightly bent to act as shock-absorbers when the ride gets bumpy, and your feet should be at a comfortable distance apart.

Once the stance is perfected for light to medium winds, it is time to start thinking about getting into the harness. The harness does more than simply take the weight off your arms – it also vastly improves the efficiency of your sailing in medium to strong winds. A downward force is generated by hanging your weight in the harness, which acts down through the mast to create the all-important 'mast-foot pressure' (MFP).

Mast-foot pressure is the key to board speed and acceleration, as it keeps the board level and trims it while planing. Once on the plane, it is mast-foot pressure that enables you to move back on the board and into the footstraps. Without it the tail would simply sink under your weight. Once you are in the footstraps the exciting new experience of footsteering becomes possible.

Figure 23 The beach-start. *(a)* Control the board's position with your front hand on the mast and the back hand on the boom. *(b)* With the board on a reach and both hands on the boom, put your back foot across the centreline. *(c)* Extend the arms to get the rig forward and upright. *(d)* Thrust the hips forward over the bent leg. *(e)* Lever down on the boom to raise the front leg, and place the front foot over the centreline.

HARNESS USE It is important to set up the lines correctly, so that when hooked in you can assume a normal sailing stance (Figure 24). Hold the rig on the beach as if you were sailing, and then move your hands as close together on the boom as you can manage. You have now found the balance point of the rig, so you can attach the harness lines at an equal distance on either side of this balance point, about a shoulder-width apart. In practice, the balance point will be slightly nearer the clew than this when on the water. When sailing, the effect of the apparent wind moves the centre of effort further aft in the sail. To compensate for this, move the lines slightly further back. A simple way of checking that your lines are correctly positioned is to take one hand off the boom while sailing and allow the harness to do most – or indeed all – of the work. If this is not possible, then the fixing positions should be adjusted immediately. This is also true for changes in wind strength. As the wind gets up the sail has to work harder, and inevitably the

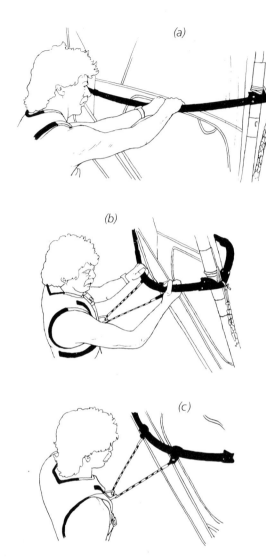

Figure 24 Harness use. *(a)* Hold the rig on the beach with your hands a shoulder-width apart. Move them together, and where they meet should be the boom's balance point. *(b)* Attach the two ends of the line, equidistant from the balance point, shoulder-width apart, and then move them a little further back to allow for the apparent wind while sailing. The lines should be short enough for your arms to be slightly bent when hooked in and sailing. *(c)* If the lines are correctly positioned, you should be able to take your hands off the boom and take the rig's weight without it twisting away.

centre of effort will move rearwards just slightly. The experienced sailor will quite possibly adjust harness-line position (and even length) many times during a sailing session to keep everything as well balanced and effortless as possible.

Harness-line length has become much shorter in recent years, owing to changes in sail and board design, and sailing technique. Lines that are too long make it more difficult to generate the necessary MFP, and can also cause the sailor inadvertently to hyperextend the back, leading to possible injury and discomfort.

FOOTSTRAP USE Planing in a strong steady wind, hooked into the harness with both feet comfortably slotted into the footstraps, is one of the great joys of windsurfing. The board can be steered simply by pressing or pushing with the feet, and is extremely responsive when turned this way. It also means that you can cruise through chop, swell and waves without the feet being swept off the board.

Footstraps are for strong winds only. If there is insufficient wind you will find it impossible to step back on the board without the tail sinking. Moving so far back on the board requires good harness technique in order to generate the necessary mast-foot pressure.

To begin with, position the footstraps as far forward as possible. This will make life much easier, and help stop you sinking the tail and luffing up too often in the early stages. Make sure that you are fully in control and that you have good board speed. The faster you are going the easier it is to move back. Take the weight off your feet by hanging in the harness so your weight is acting down through the mast foot. As you move back, the board should stay level and steady on its course. If you have too little pressure on the mast foot the board may luff up into the wind. Place your front foot first into the windward front strap, and get used to the feel. Then you can think about getting your rear foot into the back strap. When you are happy using the straps in their forward position, you can then move them back a notch or two and experience the joys of full-speed planing, and maybe even try a jump or two.

ADVANCED TECHNIQUES

Once you have mastered sailing in the foot-straps and harness, you are ready to move on to shorter boards, higher winds and a wealth of more advanced manoeuvres.

THE WATER-START The first and most important technique to be mastered is the water start (Figure 25). Uphauling a sail in winds over Force 4 is not an easy task, and the water-start makes the wind do the work for you. If the sail is presented correctly to the wind it should physically lift you from the water and straight aboard. Water-starting opens up the world of higher wind sailing, particularly for shorter boards, which have insufficient volume to allow conventional uphauling. Fortunately, it is not too difficult to learn. It is rather like riding a bike – once you have learned it, it becomes a natural, instinctive manoeuvre. You will wonder what the problem was!

The biggest problem in water-starting is holding the board and sail in the correct position. The water-start itself is the easy part of the manoeuvre, no more difficult than a deeper-water beach-start. This is the best way to learn the technique – practise beach-starting in deeper and deeper water. Once you can get going every time from chest-deep water, you are ready to go deeper.

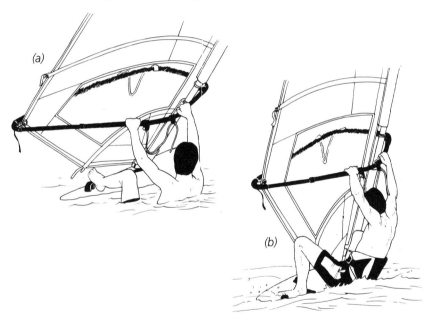

Figure 25 The water-start. *(a)* Keeping the rig well out of the water to stop the boom from catching, rest the heel of the back foot on the centreline. In light wind conditions, look for a gust and prepare to spring with an explosive arm extension. *(b)* Kick hard with the front leg which remains in the water until the last moment. Come up under the boom. Pump the sail if necessary for greater lift. *(c)* As the front foot comes up onto the board, keep the back leg bent to lower the centre of gravity, and get your weight forward as soon as possible to stop the board spinning up into wind.

SAILING SHORT BOARDS Once you have mastered harness technique, using the foot-straps and the water-start, you can in theory now sail any board of any length in just about any planing wind strength. However, everything happens much quicker on short boards, and the boards themselves are far more responsive to foot pressure. Consequently, they punish mistakes a lot quicker, and are much more technically demanding to sail. The newcomer to short boards should start on something relatively large and floaty, and only move on to smaller slalom boards and waveboards when completely comfortable on these bigger short boards.

While harness and footstrap technique, beach-starting and water-starting skills all work the same whatever the length of board, short boards have specific technique requirements. For a start, the basic turning skills of tacking and gybing have to be modified greatly. Short boards are essentially planing-only designs, so all turning manoeuvres have to be performed very quickly and smartly.

Tacking Although short-board tacking is not much different to long-board tacking, it needs to be performed as quickly as possible, and the sailor cannot put weight forward of the mast foot for any appreciable time, since the nose will sink.

The carve gybe No matter how quickly you tack, the board will still lose all speed. Consequently, the gybe is the favoured method of turning a short board, as it can be performed at full speed, and is an exhilarating manoeuvre when done correctly. Unfortunately, it is also one of the most difficult moves to learn.

Casually dipping a hand in the water during a carve gybe is a good way of ensuring that you lean into the turn.

The carve gybe. From a reach, while sailing at speed, bear away onto a broad reach and keep the speed as fast as possible. Take your rear foot out of its strap and place it further onto the leeward rail, between the front and back straps. Unhook and lean into the turn, applying pressure to the leeward rail.

As the board turns, drive forward with the knees. Extra pressure on the back foot will make the board turn even faster if required. Keep your torso upright and sheet out more as the turn progresses. Keep the board turning past the downwind position and towards the new tack.

Stage 3 *Bend the knees to counteract the pull from the rig, sheet in and power away on the new tack. Stay forward momentarily to let the board regain planing sppeed, and then step back into the footstraps and regain the harness. The whole move has taken barely a few seconds.*

Stage 2 *As the rig flips around, bring the mast upright to reposition the rig ready for the new tack. Grab the boom with the new back hand, ready to sheet in.*

Stage 1 *Bring what was your back foot forward, right up to the mast foot if necessary, to keep the tail from sinking as the board begins to slow. Either hold the sail in the clew first position for a second or two, or immediately release the back hand so the rig flips around onto the new tack.*

Whereas the water-start can be cracked in a matter of days, for most sailors the 'carve gybe' can take literally years to master. Good sailors can exit the turn almost as fast as they entered it, and crank the board through 180° on an extremely tight radius. However, some boards gybe much better than others, depending on their rocker profile, rail shape and plan shape.

Ideal learning conditions are a good Force 4–5 and flat water. Choppy water makes gybing much more difficult, as it will slow the board down and perhaps cause it to trip or bounce out. From a reach, look for an area of flat water in which to execute your turn. Bear away to gain maximum speed and unhook from the harness, but keep sheeted in with your weight outboard to keep the board flat. Once well established on a broad reach, take your rear foot out of its strap and place it towards the leeward rail, just in front of the rear strap. Lean into the turn, applying pressure to the leeward rail.

As the board turns, drive the knees forward, keeping your torso upright and your weight on the mast foot. Footsteer the board past the run position and towards the new tack. Now bring what was your back foot forward, right up to the mast foot if necessary, to keep the board flat. Either keep the sail in the clew-first position for a second or two, or release the back hand so the rig flips round onto the new tack. As it does so, be ready to take the other side of the boom with your other hand. Sheet in the sail, and sail off on a new reach.

Timing is the key to the whole exercise. Every gybe is different, affected by the wind and the water conditions, and by your own body movements. Consequently, there is no one fixed procedure that will always work. The gybe described above is a basic technique, but, depending on the conditions, the competent carve-gyber may step forward earlier or later, or increase/decrease the radius of turn to avoid a nasty piece of chop or swell.

Other turning manoeuvres Mastery of the carve gybe opens up a wide variety of high-speed turning manoeuvres. The racing or 'lay-down' gybe is an advanced variation for turning at the highest of speeds. It is a visually dramatic move in which the sailor lays the rig right down onto (but not touching) the water to dump all power from the sail, leaning into the turn as hard as possible.

The 'slam gybe', on the other hand, brings the board to an instant halt and spins it straight round onto the new tack. All speed is lost in the process, but the board turns in the tightest arc possible.

In the 'duck gybe', instead of the clew of the sail flipping round over the nose in mid-turn it is thrown over the head. The sailor ducks under the sail.

All these gybes can also be performed one-handed for extra style points. Pirouette gybes, or turns where the sail is pivoted an extra 360° on top of the basic 180° (the 'monkey gybe') do not add any functionality, but certainly look good!

There are also many variations on tacking, such as the 'duck tack' and 'helicopter tack'. Both negate the need for the sailor to stand forward of the mast, and are thus ideal for short boards.

The lay-down gybe.

The duck gybe.

APPENDIX — BEAUFORT SCALE OF WIND FORCE

Beaufort No.	Velocity in knots	General description	Sea conditions	Suitability for windsurfing
Force 0	1 or less	Calm	Calm, mirror-like	None
Force 1	1–3	Light air	Gentle scaly ripples	Good for learning, but a bit too light for most intermediates and experts
Force 2	4–6	Light breeze	Small wavelets which may have glassy crests but these will not break	Excellent for learning and relaxed cruising in the sun, and/or practising freestyle tricks
Force 3	7–10	Gentle breeze	Larger wavelets	Fine for learning on sheltered water where the wavelets are minimized; good tactical racing conditions for long boards, and the most sophisticated racing short boards can start planing
Force 4	11–16	Moderate breeze	Waves becoming larger with white horses	Boards of any length start to plane; too windy for beginners
Force 5	17–21	Fresh breeze	Moderate waves with white horses and possible occasional spray	Great for all types of short board; good for longer all-round funboards
Force 6	22–27	Strong breeze	Large waves forming with extensive white crests and spray	For competent sailors only
Force 7	28–33	Near gale	Sea heaps up and foam from breaking waves is blown in streaks	For real experts only
Force 8	34–40	Gale	Moderate to high waves; edge of crests break into spindrift	Risky, even for experts
Force 9	41–46	Severe gale	High waves; confused breaking crests	Definitely experts only!
Forces 10–12	47–55 and over	Storm/violent storm/hurricane	Exceptionally high waves hiding ships from view; sea covered in white foam	Stay at home, watching windsurfing videos and reading magazines . . .

Chop jumping.

GLOSSARY

Apparent wind A combination of the true wind and the wind created upon the sail by the board's forward motion.

Battens These are long, thin strips of fibreglass or carbon that add support to the sail, improving its stability and its aerodynamic efficiency.

Beam reach The course directly across or at 90° to the wind. This relatively fast point of sailing is also the easiest to adopt in the early stages.

Bearing away A steering manoeuvre that takes the nose of the board away from the wind.

Broad reach A reach that is further off the wind than a beam reach. On a short board (at between 110 and 130° off the wind) this is by far the fastest point of sailing. As such, it is usually adopted by high-wind-speed and slalom sailors in pursuit of Mach 1.

Camber-inducer A tuning-fork or plastic-cup type mechanism on the leading edge of the sail, fitted to sit between the mast and a batten. Together with the battens, the inducer stabilizes the front edge and luff area of the sail to make it more aerodynamically efficient.

Cavitation Sometimes called spin-out, an action that occurs when the fin becomes aerated and loses grip in the water. In practice, the back end of the board moves radically away from its track and all directional stability is lost, often resulting in a wipe-out. Someone who is a proficient sailor can recover from cavitation by various techniques to regain his or her grip, and fortunately it is not as common as it used to be, as fins have improved in quality.

Clew Region of the sail adjacent to the rear end of the boom. This reinforced area incorporates an eyelet for the outhaul rope to pass through.

Close hauled Sometimes called a beat, where the board is sailed as closely into the wind as possible to make ground upwind.

Close reach The point of sailing somewhere between a beam reach and close-hauled.

Eye of the wind The direction from which the true wind is coming.

Harness An energy-saving device that takes the strain off the sailor's arms and back, allowing longer, more efficient sailing.

Head The top area of the sail close to the mast tip.

Head-to-wind A point where the nose of the board points directly into the eye of the wind. The board has no motion and the sail flaps freely in the breeze along the board's centreline.

Heading up The opposite of bearing away – the nose of the board moves towards the wind.

Hull The windsurfing board with the rig removed.

Leech The back or trailing edge of the sail.

Planing When the board is skimming along over the surface of the water, rather than actually displacing water. There is a minimum planing wind strength of around 8–12 knots, under which there is not enough power in the sail to drive the board up onto the plane.

Rig The combination of mast, sail, boom and mast foot.

Roach The area of the sail that lies outside an imaginary line connecting the head to the clew (leech roach) and the clew to the tack (foot roach).

Run The furthest point of sailing off the wind (a complete l80°). The nose of the board points directly downwind, opposite the head-to-wind position.

Sinker Applies to short boards that will not support the dead weight of the sailor and rig when not in motion. As the term suggests, the board sinks below the surface. For experts only!

Tack The area of the sail nearest to the mast foot, reinforced and with an eyelet for the downhaul. Also a zigzagging of the board on a beat, to make ground upwind.

Universal joint The component that allows a 'freesail' system, the invention upon which the whole concept of windsurfing is based. The joint connects the rig to the board, and its mechanical or rubber structure allows the mast to be tilted in any plane about 360°.

Wipe-out That all-too-common early bath from only-too-regular pilot error!

USEFUL ADDRESSES

Royal Yachting Association

RYA House
Romsey Road
Eastleigh
Hants
SO5 4YA
Tel. 01703 629962

Professional Windsurfers' Association

21 Chelsea Wharf
15 Lots Road
London
SW10 OQJ
Tel. 0171 376 7446

United Kingdom Boardsailing Association

PO Box 36
Sarrisbury Green
Hampshire
SO3 6SB
Tel. 01489 579642

British Windsurfing Association

Mengham Cottage
Mengham Lane
Hayling Island
Hants
PO11 9JX
Tel. 01705 468182

INDEX

×××××××××××××××××××××